To my young cousin Jean De Haven in Oregon
I owe the following story, for she wrote me
on the eve of her graduation from the Oregon
College of Education a letter I have saved
and savored.

Expressing her appreciation of the things
she believes I have accomplished, Jeanie
asked, "What induced you to go into social
work in 1913, what was it like then, and
what is it like now?" A large order, which
I have to fulfill in my own way, but it
warmed this eighty-four-old heart and an-
cient typewriter into action.

Jeanie, I have tried in episodic fashion to
answer your questions, but mostly you have
driven me to look back over those sixty
years of living and of taking part in social
work to assess them and my own emerging
beliefs.

With affection, I dedicate this story to you.
                                C. M. T.

CSS building, 1890's.

CLARE M. TOUSLEY

LETTER TO JEANIE

Highlights of Sixty Years
with Social Work Professionals
and Volunteers

FAMILY SERVICE ASSOCIATION OF AMERICA
44 East 23rd Street . New York, N.Y.   10010

International Standard Book Number: 0-87304-144-5
Library of Congress Catalog Card Number: 76-16430

Printed in the United States of America

FOREWORD

Dear C.M.T.:

It gives me great pleasure to write a "foreword" for the publication by the Family Service Association of America of your *Letter to Jeanie*. The funds that have made this publication possible came from your friends, COS volunteers, and alumnae of your "Junior Month." As you know, the COS Board member who was instrumental in helping you get the "Junior Month" program off the ground was my father's oldest sister. You will recall that you and I first met when I was trying to learn something about this aunt, Mrs. John M. Glenn, after I had found through reading some old issues of *Highlights* that she had served as president of what is now FSAA from 1920 until 1936. She must have been a pretty tough old girl to survive sixteen years in that job!

So much for my confession of involuntary nepotism.

Letter to Jeanie is, of course, an interesting chronicle, presenting as it does a very human and informal picture of your experience in the development of social work in the United States, spanning the years from 1911 to 1970. Coincidentally, it was in 1911 that the Charity Organization Society created the National Association for Organizing Charities, which was later to become FSAA.

But far more than that, every page of *Letter to Jeanie* shines with the enthusiasm that you showed in devoting six decades of your life to the improvement of the lot of families--and people--in an increasingly complex society. Your own obvious satisfaction in the social work career you chose for yourself cannot help but provide inspiration for young people of good will to follow in your footsteps. Volunteers, too, can take encouragement from the many anecdotes you have related, pointing out the important results that lay people have accomplished over the years when guided by a person of your resourcefulness and energy.

To me, however, the real contribution that *Letter to Jeanie* makes to social work and the family service field is in showing how some of your experiences over the years are relevant to today's world. For example, what better illustration of what we now call "family advocacy" could there be than the efforts the president and executive director of COS made in the early 1930s in securing passage of the first tenement-house law for New York City, or in helping to create and staff the first Home Relief Department in that city, which, as you point out, was "a beginning part of the development of public welfare in our country."

Similarly, the efforts that your leaders and you devoted to the establishment of the New York School of Social Work (now the Columbia University School of Social Work) lead in a direct line to the work now being done by practitioners from family service and other agencies in providing field work practice and supervision to students from schools of social work throughout the United States and Canada.

In the family service field, there is one lesson we have learned well from you. And that is the importance of public relations. Page after page of your *Letter to Jeanie* illustrates in detail your thesis that if the public is to understand what family service, or social work for that matter, is about, then they must be shown case examples to which they can relate. Furthermore, there is a clear path from Ruth Draper's presentation of "The Dalmatian Peasant," through the Community Plays of the American Theatre Wing, to Plays for Living. This "case-to-cause" approach to meeting people's needs is one to which we subscribe as heartily as you do. *Letter to Jeanie* provides another way to get the message across!

The Family Service Association of America is deeply indebted to you for the privilege of disseminating *Letter to Jeanie* to a wider audience. It is a letter worth remembering.

H. Barksdale Brown
*President, Family Service
Association of America*

PREFACE

Someone has said that the criterion of success is influence. If that is true--and I believe it is--then there is one person about whose success there can be no doubt, Miss Clare M. Tousley. The ways in which Miss Tousley has brought her influence to bear are so many that I could not possibly list them all.

I am sure that many of you here today could tell of some small and special way in which C.M.T., as she is affectionately called, has left an indelible mark on your thinking and on your understanding of social work.

When I was a provisional member of the Junior League of New York, it was C.M.T. who first opened my eyes to the field of family service and the ways in which a green young volunteer might be helpful in this great city.

My roommate at Vassar was influenced, too. She came back excited and enthusiastic from her experience in CSS "Junior Month," when third-year students from twelve colleges spent four weeks in New York under Miss Tousley's leadership.

Young people are still being influenced by

Delivered at the CSS Women's Council Meeting, November 28, 1955, on the occasion of Miss Tousley's retirement from the Community Service Society. Typically, C.M.T. couldn't attend; she was in court testifying in behalf of a young friend.

ix

her. This very year, her teaching at the School of Social Welfare of the University of California at Berkeley so moved her class that they sent a message to the national Council on Social Work Education urging similar courses in all schools of social work.

Legion are the people, not only in New York but all over the country, who through the years have eagerly read the little CSS *Bulletin* with the familiar signature, C.M.T., and have been influenced not only to contribute to CSS but to *understand* the poignant troubles of CSS families.

Way back in 1919, Clare Tousley started to work with the volunteers who were serving the Charity Organization Society, one of the predecessor organizations of CSS. From that moment on, her warm interest in the volunteer in social work never flagged. With patience and devotion she has taught them, with charm and wit she has kept their spirits up, with dedication and knowledge she has inspired them.

Blanchette Rockefeller
(Mrs. John D. Rockefeller 3rd)

ACKNOWLEDGMENTS

If there are any errors in *Letter to Jeanie,* I will excuse the following friends who gave me stimulus and helped while my memory unwound.

I would especially like to salute the three Oberlin classmates who were at table when this story began the day we graduated in 1911. They write from California now that they still remember it all just as chronicled here. My greetings and thanks to these three lifelong friends: Mrs. Maud Merrill James, Mrs. Elliot Mears, and Mrs. Maude Stewart.

I also salute others who helped me unfold this tale, including Jean Kallenberg, Barbara King, Elsa Koskinen, Natalie Linderholm, Margaret Mangold, Dr. David Milrod, Karl de Schweinitz, and Frances Schmidt. Special thanks are due, too, to the Community Service Society's archives staff and General Director Alvin L. Schorr, who invited me to publicly share these happy reminiscences with Jeanie and those who help carry on the Society's never-ending work of helping people in distress.

C.M.T.

LETTER TO JEANIE

ear Jeanie:

You asked me to tell you how I happened to go into social work and what it's all about. Whew!

Well, I guess there are three things that made it happen, and I'll try to give you some written snapshots of these.

First, there was an episode at my 1911 graduation from Oberlin College in Ohio. We three classmates sat at lunch in our senior dorm tightly gripping our new sheepskins--Maude, Gladys, and I. We were joined by a fourth friend we called "Peter" and her father, who had come on from Minnesota to see her graduate. "Where is your father?" he asked me. "My daughter said he, too, would be here." I could not help but gulp hard to keep back the tears. I had told Peter a lie. I knew he wouldn't come, although Cleveland was only forty miles away. He had promised to come off and on all these years since he had brought me to Oberlin Prep School when I was fifteen. I gulped again and began remembering it all.

My father had explained that his new wife did not want me to mix things up. She was "sick of his divorce and those two children of his who had come to live with them," he said apologetically, adding that I surely would understand it made a problem for her. "Of course, I'll pay all your bills," he said hastily, "and don't worry, for you know I love you." He put down my suitcase on the dormitory porch, kissed me hard, and fled for the Interurban Transit to Cleveland.

This episode had a deep effect on my life and my entry into social work. In retrospect it even had its humorous side. After my father fled, I found my way upstairs to my room. There were two cots but no roommate. Suddenly she came in-- two years older than I and most attractive. Her name, she said, was Gladys Iddings. She had heard me crying my heart out, so dashed in from the hallway. "Dear me," she said, "please don't cry; everything will be all right." But my sobs continued unabated, for I couldn't stop them. I honestly felt I did not want to live any longer.

Then Glad said, "I know what we'll do. When I left home in Kendallville, Indiana, my mother gave me this bottle filled with elderberry wine she had made. 'Use it,' she told me, 'when you have cramps or when there is a crisis of some kind.' I guess this is a crisis," Glad said, "so let's both have a little."

She poured out two fairly sizeable portions (not knowing that Oberlin was so dry in 1907 that instant expulsion could be expected), and we gulped it down. Her concern for me, as well as the wine, had an almost immediate effect. I felt wanted and welcome as I dried the tears and we went downstairs to supper with boys and girls who ate together. Glad introduced me all around. I reached out for companionship, and before long a new life was opened up to me at Oberlin. My student friends became my home and family--an attitude I have continued to feel all my life.[*]

But to go back to Peter's father, Mr. Merrill, who overlooked my absorption in all these memories, and my failure to answer his question about my father. He said not a word. He just patted my hand and then posed a question to all of us.

"So what are you three going to do now that you have your B.A.'s?" Like a Greek chorus we replied, "We have to get jobs right away; probably teaching is all there is." Mr. Merrill, with a Santa Claus air, asked: "How would you three like to come to Minnesota to work? I have three jobs to offer." "Sure, we'd love to," we chorused. "What would we do?"

He leaned back in the creaky dormitory chair and drew this picture: "Our State Institution for Dependent Children is on the outskirts of a little town. The courts send these children to us for care and adoption because they have found their parents to be improper guardians. We have about 300 boys and girls under fourteen right now. Some are easy to find adoptive homes for, but many stay a long time waiting, especially if they are handicapped in some way."

"Then what would our jobs be?" we asked. "I'm coming to that," he said. "First we need someone to travel around the state taking the

---

[*]My cup of gratitude to Oberlin ran over when, in June 1937, I was invited back to receive an honorary LL.D. degree as "a beloved daughter of Oberlin marking her achievement in social work."

3

children for whom adoptive homes have been found to these families."

"I'd like that one" Maude piped up. "I like children. I like to travel."

"Good enough," he said, "so now for the second job. This needs someone who is musical, who knows how to run a library, and who can act as principal of our grade school when called on."

"That's you, Glad," we said. "Look how you play the violin, and then there was that library course you took during your junior year. You could easily lead the children in singing, and why not fill in as 'Lady Principal' with that dignified New England way of yours?" "Settled," said Peter's father.

So I piped up and asked what was left for me to do, to which he replied: "Teach the first grade."

"All right," I assented, but with some trepidation when he told me it would be a sort of ungraded class of children from about ages six to thirteen because many had had no schooling, especially those from the remote Canadian border region. "You won't have the same children all the time," he added, "for every week some will go out for adoption, new ones come in, and therefore, it won't be as formal an assignment as regular teaching."

"Oh, you can do that," my classmates chimed in encouragingly, "and you can help Glad with the singing at the Sunday Chapel Hour, for you were song leader here at college all last year, and you can play the guitar and mandolin."

"So it's all settled?" queried Mr. Merrill.
"All right, I'll have a two-room suite ready for
you three girls at the top of the Administration
Building when you arrive September 1." Peter
was aglow with her father's whole idea. "You'll
be near us too," she said, "for our house is
just at the foot of the hill below the children's
cottages."

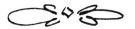

September 1 was bound to arrive and so were
we. The Minnesota autumn was beginning to show
color, and the little Straight River, which was
in fact quite crooked, bubbled along not far away.

Saturday mornings while Maude was on her
trips with the children, Glad and I were loaned
Peter's canoe to paddle "down the river aways"
and cook breakfast. Glad, who had chosen that
course in library work, also had taken one in or-
nithology. So on that river bank we relaxed from
work, and I learned to identify forty birds and
their cheerful songs before the year was over.
I still think of Glad when a rose-breasted gros-
beak sings to me up in Connecticut.

School went tolerably well after I got used
to the comings and goings of thirty to forty
children, many of whom showed the hungers and
angers of children cut adrift from their homes.
In fact, Glad and I decided the best thing to
do was to give them a good time and try to make
up for some of their loss. So we burst forth
with such ideas as trips up the river to learn
about birds while picnicking there and going

to the circus when it came to town. It worked,
so we cooked up more ideas. A glee club was
formed; and meantime, we two, all costumed and
blacked up to hide our identities, journeyed,
complete with instruments on Saturday nights,
from cottage to cottage to sing with the children. I can still see them in their nighties
sitting in a circle eagerly waiting for "Mr. and
Mrs. Bonehead" to arrive.

Maybe it was my own broken-home background,
Jeanie, that made me want so much to help heal
these children's hurts, for I had not yet mended
my heart. This, I guess, was a deep impulse later toward social work.

Secondly, an episode in class that February
was, I think, an invisible launching pad toward
social work. Stocky little Adolf, age eight,
came in one Friday beamingly announcing: "I'm
going to a home tomorrow. I'm going to have a
mother." I found myself with two sets of feel-
ings--pleasure and anxiety--for this little boy
had found a place in my heart, and I did not
want him hurt again if things went wrong. It
was only a week later in fact that Glad said as
she looked out our bedroom window while dressing
for breakfast, "Oh dear, look who's coming up
the hill with his little gray laundry case in
hand!"

Yes, there he was, accompanied by one of
the institution's "agents." "What on earth do
you suppose has gone wrong?" I exploded to Glad.
"And what will I say to him when he comes to
class this morning?" I didn't need to plan it,
because when he arrived he put his head on the
desk and would not respond to any approach I
could think of.

Two days passed by this way, and finally near the end of the second one I felt desperate. "Adolf," I said, "would you be willing to stay after school and help me? While you were gone a mouse has been eating our erasers and I'm scared of him. He came out of that hole over there by the chalk cupboard."

My heart pounded with hope when I saw the little boy wait until the others had gone home to their cottages.

But he couldn't look up at me until he asked: "What shall I catch him with if he comes?" "Just take your cap," I said, "and sit down on the floor by the hole and wait."

He did and I'm sure I sent up a prayer to the "God of Good Mice." For sure enough, Mr. Mouse came out. Adolf grabbed him excitedly and said, "What should I do with him?" "Run across the road to the cornfield," I said, "and turn him loose. He won't come back again, for he's learned his lesson."

There was a rush to the outside door, and shortly Adolf was back sans mouse. I called him to me and slowly he came and stood beside my desk. Putting my arm around him, I said, "Tell me, darling, what happened that hurt you so?"

An upheaval of feelings, like a small earthquake, trembled within him. Can I bring them to the surface as I want to, I thought--and I kissed him.

The dikes broke and the tears flooded forth as he said: "She didn't like me. She didn't want me." I held him tightly, and we both cried

7

until I could say: "No, that couldn't be so, Adolf, for you are very lovable. Something must have been the matter with her, not you. There's some explanation, and I will go right up to the office and find out. In the morning, please come early to class and I'll tell you."

So, Jeanie, the nutshell story was that the farm family thought he was eighteen, not eight; and since they wanted a farmhand and not a little boy, they sent him back. I think the whole world rolled off his little shoulders as I told him, and glory be, at recess there he was the same rollicking little boy he had been before.

A nice true story this one, and by April he had gone to another home that had been carefully chosen. The reports that were given to us told me I need not worry about him any more. He had a mother who wanted him. However, throughout the spring, I worried about this whole process of child adoption and drastic court decisions.

When school ended in June, I accepted a relaxing summer-camp job in Maine in surroundings so wonderfully different from Detroit and Cleveland, where I'd been brought up. An Oberlin roommate, Clarissa, who lived in New York, had spotted this chance for me, and I never went back to Minnesota again, but moved in with her Brooklyn family that fall.

I recall well, after filling temporary, dull jobs, that in December 1912 I went to the Intercollegiate Bureau of Occupations, which had just opened that week in New York. When they asked about my work interests, I said, "I want a job to help people." Frances Cummings, the Bureau's head, looked through her beginning list of openings and said: "On the strength of your letter from Minnesota I think I can recommend you for a two-week substitute position as a caseworker with the Charity Organization Society across the street."

I was delighted, and on December 23 I found myself assigned to the Riverside District Office up on the hill near Columbia University. The District Director was Miss Johanna Bojesen, who, at that time, seemed sort of scary and "executive-like."

That first day I had hoped to get home early for a Christmas Eve celebration of my December 25 birthday. Instead, at five o'clock Miss Bojesen came in to say: "I'm sorry to send you out on an emergency, but there's nobody else to go. You don't need to know anything about the case except it's a single woman in a rooming house who says she is being put out tomorrow for nonpayment of rent. We have a record about her, but you just go over to 110th Street and give her this card to a convalescent home where she can stay without charge for two weeks--if she's really to be dispossessed. Here's the carfare for her."

I bundled up against the blinding snowstorm, found the rooming house and the "single lady" wearing a red dressing gown. She confirmed that she was being put out the next day. "And you," she said rather dramatically, "will, I'm sure, be celebrating Christmas with your family or friends."

Quickly I pulled out the reference card and explained that she would be well taken care of at St. Eleanora's Home. "Have you ever been there?" she queried, looking over the card. I had to say no, of course, and this brought on the ejaculation that "a dog wouldn't go there." Her tears flowed, and finally she said: "Tomorrow you can think of me in the river; this is the end!"

I was horrified and looked at my watch; it was six o'clock. The office was closed; there was nobody to consult. Then I had a Christmas

10

Eve inspiration. The night before, my college roommate's brother-in-law had challenged me to spinning three $10 gold pieces, one of which would be mine if I won. I did, but said to him in my middle western way that "I don't gamble." He howled with laughter and said: "You work for the poor, don't you? Well then, if you are so noble, give it away," which I did, to the single lady. I explained that the Charity Organization Society surely would not approve, but it was *my* $10 and I couldn't face Christmas unless she was cared for over the weekend until someone could decide on a course of action.

All the way home to Spuyten Duyvil, where the family was then living, my anger rose inside. "What a way to treat people," I kept thinking. Everyone was finishing dinner when I arrived and burst forth with my story. They quickly agreed it must be a horrible organization, and my roommate added: "You know the head of the publishing house where I work is on their Board. I'll bet he doesn't know the half of what goes on over there, and I will tell him."

Shortly after I arrived at the Riverside District Office Monday morning, Miss Bojesen came to my desk and said briefly that I was wanted at once down on 22nd Street at our Central Office. During the subway ride down I recalled that the publishing-house head might already have been told about the fiasco. Oh dear, I'd lose my job of $10 a week. I had little money left and no family to turn to if I was fired.

Soon I was ushered into the private office of the General Director, Frank Persons (later head of the American Red Cross during World War I).

"I understand," he said rather formally, "that you disagreed with the assignment given you on December 24 and that you reported it all so that it reached our Board member, Mr. Charles Merrill. He has just been over here quite exercised about this case. Will you tell me in your own words just what happened, please?"

Quaking inside, I told it all. Mr. Persons excused himself to make a private call to Miss Bojesen. When he returned, he said that they both agreed it was a little hard on a new worker to face such a situation and that he would keep me for the two weeks' employment if I thought that any further upsets I might have would be explained to the District Director or to him-- and not the Board of Directors.

I heaved a big sigh of relief, boarded the subway, and crept back into the Riverside District Office on tiptoe hoping not to be seen. But out came Miss Bojesen. "Please come into my office," she said. Inwardly trembling, I followed her and sat down beside her desk. I was surprised and relieved when she announced right away that the blame was really hers. Then in her charming Danish way that I came later to admire so much, she leaned over and patted my cheek, saying: "You're such a dear, silly little ass. Now, go read the record of the lady in the rooming house." Quite a story it was of an English burlesque actress who had pulled several similar "fast ones" on the public.

So it was I stayed the two weeks, took some training later at the New York School of Philanthropy, and remained with the Society (now Community Service Society) for forty-three years in nineteen different positions, including Assistant General Director of COS.

So, Jeanie, that is how I got into social work, preconditioned for it, I'm sure, by my own broken home, by Adolf's and other children's loneliness in Minnesota, and by a lucky break that got me into social work when it was in its infancy in 1913. Lucky all along the way, I was especially so in 1917 when I was given a year's time by COS to attend and graduate from the New York School of Philanthropy, which later became the Columbia University School of Social Work. It was small and informal but with giants of faculty headed by that unforgettable Porter R. Lee. His gentle philosophy, intellectual depth, and unfailing humor certainly eased the learning process. And can any ex-student forget the whipped cream he occasionally offered us when the going was hard, in the form of side-splitting monologues, for instance, "The Man in the Upper Berth."

So it is the quality of leadership that counts wherever one studies--right, Jeanie?

Now as to what social work is all about to-day, as you ask. It is very different--but that's for a later chapter, so let's go back to 1913.

Not long after the $10-gold-piece episode, Miss Bojesen was summoned with others of the staff to help the Red Cross handle victims of a devastating midwest flood. She departed hurriedly, leaving me, of all people, in temporary charge of the office now that my substitute two weeks were extended.

Her final breezy instructions were: "(1) Take good care of the cash box, and put in it a list of all relief grants made during my absence; (2) Be sure that Mr. Smith does not desert his family--he is doing pretty well now; (3) I will bring my bowl of prize goldfish to the office with the food and instructions. Take good care of them."

Three weeks later, when she returned from the flood-relief work, Miss Bojesen at once called me in. "Oh, yes," I said, "all had gone well." Had Mr. Smith deserted? Oh, but no; he was on his new job already. She looked at me squarely and then said, "Your eyes are always a dead giveaway. Something went wrong--probably the cash box was stolen; anyway you might as well tell me."

So I blurted out the truth about the fish, hating to hurt her, for she cherished Peter, Stevie, and Charlie, as she called them. I recounted how they had all suddenly died and I was floored. I tucked their bodies into an office envelope and raced to a Harlem fish store. I told the proprietor how much they meant to my boss and that he must match them with live ones so she'd never know. He and I had gone to the big tank at the back of the store where he dipped and dipped until we both felt he had selected duplicates. These duplicates, I told her, were now in a little back room with the windows open, for he had reported that the fish had suffocated over the weekend.

She darted to see them. Yes, sir, there they were, swimming about happily in her bowl. Encouraged by the sound of her laughter, I joined her. "Well, this confirms what I told Mr. Persons about your qualifications before I left," she said, "initiative, imagination, and responsibility; now I guess I'll have to tell him the story of the goldfish."

So she did, and at the farewell party given him later on when he left to head the National Red Cross in Washington, the Board and staff learned from him about the matched goldfish. By that time I had begun to grow up, but I was never allowed to hear the last of the goldfish or the $10 gold piece.

In 1914 I was promoted to a semi-executive post at our Greenwich Village branch office and shortly thereafter was given half-time off with pay to study for a social science M.A. at Columbia University. Returning to the Greenwich Village office later as District Director, I eagerly attended local professional meetings as well as state welfare conferences to deepen my understanding of what casework was striving to accomplish with people and what methods could bring best results.

Certainly our hearts were in the right place, but as I look back I know that we faltered too often because we tried to do things *to* and *for* people, not *with* and *through* them as is today's professional procedure. Yes, we were pretty naive, and so was social work. But, after all, that was sixty years ago.

In 1915 came a wonderful summer opportunity which, student that you are, Jeanie, you will see the value of for me. Dr. Edward T. Devine, then General Director of the Society, recommended me to what is now Family Service Association of America. We were to join with caseworkers from nineteen other cities to study with the founder of the casework method, Mary E. Richmond of Baltimore. She was working on her forthcoming book, *Social Diagnosis,* later to become required reading for all social work students.

As I read it now I can hear her again vigorously expostulating her premise that people should not be helped as categories such as deserted wives, the unemployed, and the homeless, but as people--case by case--each one different from the other and needing individual understanding and differentiated help.

Yet I am a bit ashamed of "my page" in the book as I read it over now. It vividly illustrates one big weakness of that beginning period. Today in getting to understand your client you wouldn't go to his former employer for an evaluation or talk to the neighbors at previous addresses. None of this at least without its being the client's expressed wish. It was a well-meant bit of semi-detective work, not punitive like political witch-hunting. It sometimes threw light, but our profession knows now that it is the family's direct participation in the helping and planning process that is essential if problems are to be solved. The initiative needs always to remain with the client and not be superimposed.

But Miss Richmond saw also the other side of today's family service coin--the need for social action to improve conditions that lie back of family problems. What kind, you ask? Well, slums, for example, and imprisonment of juvenile offenders with adult ones. In fact, Miss Richmond spoke with pride of our Society's successful fight in 1915 to establish for the first time a separate Children's Court and a probation system for the young.

When I pass by that Court building today at 135 East 22nd Street, I think back on the many times I represented young people there before various judges, and of once being escorted out to the street by an officer because I differed openly and vigorously with the judicial decision.

After Miss Richmond's institute in 1915, I returned to our Greenwich Village District and tried to put into practice some of the things I had learned from her and from that wise man, Francis McLean, who assisted her, as well as from the other nineteen city representatives.

Later that winter, although not knowing

much about proper eating and cooking, I did have one startling flight of fancy unrelated to social diagnosis. It changed my professional life as it turned out. Our office in a brownstone Village house owned by Trinity Church had beautiful ground-floor rooms with fireplaces. A number of the nearby families we were helping came from MacDougal and Sullivan Streets, largely Italian then.

We had been worried about some of their undernourished children sent off to school sustained largely by black coffee and a bun. So one morning around the cozy fireplace in my office, we gave a Saturday breakfast party to twelve of these charming little boys and girls. From the kitchen downstairs we produced a menu of prunes and orange juice, hot oatmeal with plenty of milk and sugar, and, of course, buns. Afterwards, we all sang songs of the upcoming Christmas season. Then one of the children asked, "Who is the little carved Italian lady on the mantelpiece?" So I told them about the exquisite shop she came from in Rome. "What's her name?" another boy asked. I suggested at once that we all give her a name since she had none. Many choices were shouted out--Angelina, Maria, and others. A decision was hard, so with a bit of help from me, we named her, midst shouts of laughter, "Prunella Oatmela."

I remember telling our Central Office Assistant Director, Karl de Schweinitz, about the hilarious event next day, with the result that I was asked to write up Prunella Oatmela for the *Bulletin* to contributors that Karl had just initiated. Then the story was used in the press, and overnight I was an author with an invitation to tell our Board members about our Greenwich

Village children. This led to writing many another *Bulletin* and using the case-story method
to interpret our work to Trustees and other
laymen.

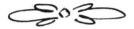

It seemed to fill a need, so in 1919 I was
promoted to a newly created position at headquarters as Karl's assistant, with the assignment of developing the *Bulletin* as a weekly
pocket-size organ to contributors.

I sorely missed Karl's help when he left
shortly to be the head of our sister-society in
Philadelphia, for I was next asked to write up
our work for the newspapers. However, I wel-
comed the chance, for I knew this could be pivotal in teaching the public new concepts of
helping people out of trouble to replace unin-
formed cliché attitudes.

So I went forth to see a few city editors
for guidance. I remember particularly the ones
at the old *Morning World,* the *New York Sun,* and
the *Evening Mail.* They were wonderful to this
novice, whose opening remark was that the public had a right to know what we were up to.
They promised help if I would submit a few news
and feature stories after I had studied their
papers. Subsequently, some of my releases were
published after considerable surgery on the
first few.

Then I decided it was my turn. I proposed
that before they would print a lurid story about

a poor family, giving names, addresses, and intimate information, they ask the reporters to phone me because often we knew them. I explained that such publicity might be a terrible setback to their lives just as constructive moves were getting under way. I gave them a recent illustration of one such family where curiosity seekers had entered the home railing at the jobless, bewildered father and distraught mother and children. The next day the husband took his life.

Out of these press overtures there grew some important two-way learning. Maybe a drop in the bucket, one might say, but fewer buckets and lives went to the bottom of the well, I believe.

From the very start the press liked the feature-story material about people we helped. These "for-example" stories were vivid and believable largely because, with minor editing, they were often written by our social work district reporters. I had early discovered that practitioners in most professions, including social work, used technical language which could throw the public. So from our nine district offices, one from each was chosen to attend our writing clinics. They learned a lot about the citizens' right to know how we helped people in their stead. The district reporters began to produce compelling stories from their grass-roots experiences. The best were used with the newspapers or published in our *Bulletin* to contributors over the initials of the reporter-author, and for the *New York Times*'s Neediest Cases Fund.

Some of these staff members then began to try public speaking about their work, so I drew them a chart around the capital letter "H" to help them give an audience a visual picture of our agency. "The left bar," I explained, "is casework and is attached to the right bar, community action, the two historical functions of COS. The cross bar, representing social research, connects the two. Thus, the need for community action coming from casework evidence can be researched and pulled together."

The "H" chart was also useful shortly thereafter when I was asked to draw up and head a volunteer program for Junior League members and other lay recruits to help us as aides in the district offices after we gave them some training. It was very exciting to see them take hold and learn about the needs of people "from the other side of the tracks."

"Should we not recruit some men volunteers?" I asked the group one day. The idea did not fall on deaf ears, for the next night I was aroused from sleep by a volunteer who excitedly phoned saying, "I am dancing with the most divine man, and he is terribly excited about what I am doing. Can you see him tomorrow at 9 a.m.?" "Indeed, yes, and what is his name?" "Oh, yes, it is John D. Rockefeller 3rd, not long out of Princeton."

Next day while mopping a perspiring forehead, John's shyness did not keep him from asking many penetrating questions about the Society and its work. In the end he joined our Boys Bureau, concerned with young men sixteen to twenty-one who were in trouble. When I later took this committee, mostly young lawyers, over to see the city's outmoded reformatory, hoping to shock them into helping us work for reform, John was one who was most upset.

"Why they're just like any little boys," he said with anguish. "Aren't there things that should be done toward changing such methods?" he asked. There were, and he did a significant part of it himself by helping us amass case information and get it written into proper form. *Youth in the Toils* was the result.

It is really John's book. Another volunteer of ours, Blanchette Hooker, who later became his wife, showed equal sensitivity and concern for people. In February 1973, John D. 3rd's book *The Second American Revolution* was published by Harper and Row, written, he says in the foreword, "with signal help from Blanchette."

Having seen them off and on since these early days, I sent my congratulations especially because the book describes my own philosophy about the influential citizen leadership needed to bring change in America. "Whether we achieve a higher level of human existence or descend to anarchy and despair depends on how well we learn to influence change in positive directions," he writes.

In acknowledging my praise of the book, Blanchette replied in part: "I have read your letter to John reminiscing about his interest in prison reform and the long hours he spent working with others over writing *Youth in the Toils*. We thank you for your thoughtfulness and send our best wishes and affection."

22

Sailor suits all the rage in 1909

Jeanie on the family farm — 1964

First Times release in 1918

Oberlin Academy 1907

"Tige" with Freshman
Classmates

Skating at
Gaitors Rink

Staff merger discussion at C. O. S.

*Bulletins for our
contributor partners*

Oberlin Honorary degree
with President Nielson
of Smith College

Hard to say
goodbye to CSS
in 1955

Social workers who have the privilege of learning how to help people have, I feel, a prime responsibility to help business and other citizen leaders to understand what we find makes human beings get into trouble, and what differentiated help each one needs. Coequal in importance, we can prove what changes in social conditions are needed for sounder family living. As the most effective champions of social change, these leaders need our firsthand facts and illustrations.

So the volunteer program that Mr. Rockefeller joined brought many other promising young men and women in touch with the realities of our city. It started off so encouragingly, in fact, that one of the Society's leading Board members, Mrs. John M. Glenn, with whom I worked, went to the Trustees with an idea for an even broader approach. Thanks to her, "Junior Month" was born, and I am still proud of being its midwife.

We chose twelve mostly women's colleges*

_____
*Barnard, Bryn Mawr, Connecticut College for Women, Elmira, Goucher, Mt. Holyoke, Radcliffe, Smith, Swarthmore, Vassar, Wellesley, and Wells.

to be in it after Mrs. Glenn had interested another Trustee, Miss Annie B. Jennings, in underwriting the project financially.

Beginning in 1919, twelve juniors from the twelve colleges came to New York each year for the month of July, where they lived, worked, learned, and played together, with their expenses covered by the Jennings scholarship. Each autumn the new aspirants were interviewed, and later one was chosen by the faculty-student committees at each college. They were selected on a competitive basis depending on their interest, educational ability, and leadership qualities. The only commitment each winner had was to return to college her senior year and report at such classes as psychology, economics, and sociology, and to speak at Chapel about her exciting summer experiences of learning.

The New York press described this as "learning what page 89 in sociology meant in terms of tenement life in the big city." The Juniors were encouraged also to report back to their hometowns in August, to their families and friends, their churches, and their local press. What did they do during those four weeks in New York? They visited our social work clients, got acquainted with the family, and often took the children to be outfitted for summer camp if mothers were busy working and then put them on trains and buses. Regularly they reported back to their district supervisors about the parents' worries concerning health problems, housing conditions, and many other family pressures. The Juniors were appalled by the congested quarters they saw and marvelled that mothers could keep their homes as tidy as they did.

Many a night we had informal seminars about what they saw and did that day or week. Some of New York's finest leaders met with them for lively discussions and guidance in their earnest search for possible change and reform. Housing officials, psychiatrists, probation officers, and settlement house workers were among those who came. There were questions galore, answers galore far into the night sometimes.

As a recess from problems we went off over weekends in a body to visit Board members like Miss Jennings in their country homes, not only for relaxation, but because I saw our Society as a team of Board, staff, and volunteers, which concept they could understand by getting closer to it.*

The Juniors hurled some provocative findings at their Trustee-hosts, which gave these leaders some fresh firsthand impressions that were healthy, even if upsetting at times. One noon, I recall, we went down to lunch with Walter S. Gifford, head of American Tel and Tel, in his office dining room overlooking the Statue of Liberty and the bay.

A New England kind of man, brilliant and diffident, he loved it when one student asked, "Mr. Gifford, how did you get this job?" He replied in amusement: "Well one day when I wrote to the General Electric Company from Harvard Business School, seeking an opening, I put the letter by mistake in an envelope addressed to the Western Electric Company. Their reply

*I recall especially happy visits to the homes of Robert de Forest and his son, Johnston, as well as a delightful weekend with the Russell Leffingwells and the Richard S. Childs.

asked me to make up my mind and I did--the
Western Electric Company."

Of course, the students included this story and other such gems during their Chapel reports back at college. They did well at this
reporting, albeit sometimes the hard way. Before the Bryn Mawr Junior got into her Chapel
talk one year, she panicked. Glaring angrily
at the faculty and students before her, she
said, "I refuse to go on until my knees stop
shaking." The roar of laughter helped her.
She laughed too and proceeded to give one of
the best summations of "Junior Month" ever
delivered.

Young, eager, idealistic, and charming
they were, and during those years until the big
depression ended the project after 1932, most
of the 156 Juniors gained a lifelong impetus
toward understanding and helping their fellow
men. A great many of them went into social
work professionally; others joined Boards of
agencies back home or volunteered after their
marriages, about which work they wrote me from
far-flung places. They later told their children many tales of "Junior Month" as these
youngsters started off on their own college
careers.

A rewarding, fun part of my life it was,
Jeanie, to have 156 such "children" of my own
to try to steer into deeper awareness and belief in life with all its wonderful variances.
They saw all parts of the Society's work as having one common denominator, not class or color
or income, but just people. It was good to
learn how the experience and its aftermath

later helped them in their own lives as well as in helping others.

These memories of the "Junior Months" take me back to another project that gave me added conviction that young people want to learn about their fellow man and help him. This time it was even younger women, debutantes at the Junior League, whom I addressed one day in 1924 at a session of a course for provisional members.

I had real misgivings the next year about accepting the League's invitation to speak again because, after I had met with the Provisionals the year before, I learned that the next speaker said that volunteer training was not necessary for social work, only goodwill and friendliness. So I refused their request. At the Society's headquarters, we had already started a Volunteer Training Program, in part created by the volunteers themselves, in which they emphasized the necessity for training and preparation.

When I was pressed by the Junior League about my reasons for refusal, I at first hedged, but their middle-aged League officer pursued the matter. She asked how I knew that ten months from now I'd be too busy to come on that given day. Yes, I must accept, she insisted, for I had "esprit, elan, and eclat."

I wasn't sure what all that added up to, but then I blurted out the truth, asking, "How do you put your twelve-week course together anyway?" Well, different Board members selected people from their favorite charities. I commented that this system was hard on their Provisionals, for they would get unrelated and maybe conflicting information and advice, as in my case last year. Well, then, how did I think the course should be planned?

My considered suggestion was that they select a director of the course from some names I could give them, since such a professional would protect the Board, too, from criticism. The following week I was asked to come up and prepare such a course and direct it. When I demurred, they said they would then give up the suggestion I offered. So in 1926 I started, and proud I was of these debutantes, right from the beginning.

A few of the speakers I chose--especially blacks--and some of the field trips I took the Provisionals on--to children's courts and reformatories--scared a few mothers. And why not? This was a half century ago when today's city realities had not surfaced. But the Provisionals settled this one on their first final exam. They gave top preference to the black minister --no Uncle Tom--to whom they tossed such questions as intermarriage between races.

They liked his answering with directness and humor. One time he said, "Marriage for everybody is a challenge, and if you add differences like this to be overcome, success is just that much harder."

Those twenty years of teaching at the League from 1926 to 1946 are still precious memories, as is that of the final luncheon, Ginnie,* given me there as a warm goodbye, highlighted by their gift of Honorary Life Membership. My greatest pride, however, is knowing what these and other young volunteers did with their "come-and-see-and-learn" experience.

A good by-product resulted when Barnard College heard about this annual course at the Junior League and I was allowed by our Board to accept their invitation to teach once weekly to seniors a series called "Introduction to Social Work." For four years in the late twenties, through lectures, discussion, and field trips, these students were able to use the resources of New York City as their campus. They loved getting theory and reality blended when after each field trip we sat down together in some nearby spot and discussed what they had just seen and heard, such as hearings at the Children's Court.

Years later, in 1955, I adopted this method when teaching a summer course at the University of California at Berkeley School of Social Welfare. The emphasis here was on communications and how to tell what the students knew and saw to a public that too often failed to understand through sheer distance from such problems.

*Mrs. Garret J. (Virginia) Garretson 2nd, then president of the Junior League and later president (1960-66) of CSS.

Sometime in the Roaring Twenties, as they were called by the press, just as I was starting out on my annual visits to the twelve "Junior Month" colleges, I went on a roaring rebellion of my own. I guess this was rebellion number two, not unlike the $10-gold-piece one of 1912.

I had heard that our cold fish of a three-hour-for-lunch fund-raiser (appropriately named Mr. Snow), who knew little and cared less about family casework, had recommended to the Board that our Bronx District Office be closed down for lack of funds. I had worked in the Bronx briefly the summer before and remembered well the families we were helping, and I blew up loudly about the proposal.

Next day I was summoned to explain my vociferous objections to the Society's president, Robert W. de Forest. It was a breakfast invitation to his lovely house at 7 Washington Square North. While waiting for him to appear, I looked around the room and saw masterpiece paintings that left me breathless. I knew Mr. de Forest was president of the Metropolitan Museum of Art, the Russell Sage Foundation, and other distinguished bodies, but here was a veritable museum before my eyes.

It was hard after that to get started explaining my rebellion. But while breakfast was being served to us, I gave our president story after story about our Bronx clients, urging that an important Society like ours should not abandon them. Surely, with the kind of Trustees we had, the needed $80,000 could be raised to avert the closing.

The next week, at Mr. de Forest's request, I found myself telling it all over again to the Board of Trustees. He then announced to them that he would lead a drive to raise the money if they would agree to help, adding that he would ask me to assist them. I protested that I knew nothing about fund-raising, but, headlong, I was launched into it.

Success came, thanks to Mr. de Forest and his tremendous following. There was a usual finale of congratulations all around. Next day I had a visitor. It was the liveried chauffeur of "R.W.," as we called him, bearing a note attached to a package. The note read, "Dear C.M.T. --you won!" The package contained a beautiful jade pin from Tiffany's. I could have wept with surprise and pleasure.

Yet the next day I could have wept for another reason, for I was asked to accept the dubious post of becoming half-time fund-raiser to fit in with "Junior Month" and running our Volunteer Bureau. I assured R.W. and my boss that I would be a flat failure of ignorance. But to no avail. They said I couldn't be worse than Mr. Snow, who had already been melted out.

I discovered early, however, that by providing ammunition to the Trustees, this case method of evidence was an important magnet for them to use in getting voluntary giving. It also gave the Board members themselves knowledge that helped them more realistically to fulfill their trusteeship role. They needed to know more about causes of trouble and were heartened by results of their efforts toward bringing help to broken lives.

So we began using this interpretive tool of "bearing witness" to all our contributors via the *Bulletin* and by our letters signed by the Board. I felt that we were building an army, not just of givers, but of believers. Contributions were more often renewed annually, and also bequests grew out of donor communication.

Most of their letters had been moving and serious, but I remember one funny one. This contributor sent a personal note with his check praising the last issue of the *Bulletin,* and he asked what my initials C.M.T., as editor, stood for.

I replied that it would cost him $1,000 more for me to reveal my first name. Back came the $1,000, but then he wanted to know what the "M" stood for. Just for fun I wrote him that this information would require $2,000 more at least. Sure enough it came, with such an amusing note wanting to know if I had any other names. I answered that I did have a college nickname still too widely used, but that such a revelation would cost $5,000. Apparently this intrigued him even more, and he sent the $5,000.

It was all a fun episode which had a comical surprise ending. The donor, who was Mr. Simmons of the Simmons Bed Company, later called up to express his pleasure in this game we played to benefit COS. Then he asked me if I could get our president, Mr. de Forest, to have his picture taken standing beside one of their beds. I explained in horror that I could not ask this dignified representative of many of New York's leading causes to do any such thing. "I guessed as much," he said resignedly.

Later that week, when I was breakfasting with our president at his home, he said, "You know, C.M.T., last night I slept the best I have in months on one of those Simmons mattresses I just bought." The scrambled eggs fell off my fork. I took a deep gulp of hot coffee and said to myself, "No, I just can't, I just can't, but isn't it killing?"

Some years later--on the more serious side --can I ever forget the twenty-five dollar donation I spied in a letter from the great actress Julia Marlowe, who had long since retired from the famous husband-and-wife team of Sothern and Marlowe? The results of her twenty-five dollar contribution, reported in a personal letter from Walter Gifford, led to a second gift and then, three months later at her death, to a bequest of a third of a million dollars.

I believe the Society's records, if reviewed today, would show third- and fourth-generation descendants of famous New Yorkers still giving, because the case-by-case method gave them faith in us. This steadfastness of support was hearteningly tested as we reeled from the impact of the Wall Street crash in 1929.

The big depression descended on America and affected everything we did. The promising roars of the financial boom became frightening whimpers until the country slowly gained its equilibrium later on.

Our COS Fiftieth Annual Report of 1931-32, which I prepared for our officers, tells our part in New York's valiant attempt, through its leading citizens, to cope. Lucky we were, Jeanie, that Walter S. Gifford, president of American Tel and Tel, was our vice president, for on May 6, 1931, Robert W. de Forest, who had been our president since 1889, died. A dynamic citizen leader right to the end, he was praised and mourned by so many. His fearless and generous use of his prestige had led to the birth and strengthening of many needed causes in our city. I remember going over the list as I wrote his obituary for the press.

So many vivid memories of stories he had told me came to mind. For instance, the time he put on his silk top hat and went up to Albany to see his Cold Spring Harbor friend and neighbor, Governor Theodore Roosevelt, with the appalling findings of bad housing in his pocket.

Result No. 1:   A state commission appointed by the Governor to look into these.   Result No. 2:   The creation of the first city Tenement House Department in the country.   Result No. 3: The passage of the first tenement-house law, the forerunner of the Multiple Dwelling Law in which our distinguished COS Executive Director Lawson Purdy played such an important part, leading to city zoning and administrative reforms.

These spectacular successes toward better housing for city dwellers formed part of the program for our Fiftieth Anniversary Celebration on November 30, 1932, at Town Hall.   Our contributors, along with other friends and the press, packed the house that day.

I had been able to entice our contributor Ruth Draper, the unforgettable monologist, to present her moving sketch, "The Dalmatian Peasant," to the audience with our new President Gifford presiding.   It was the story of a non-English-speaking immigrant whose sick husband had been taken from home in an ambulance.   She could not find where he was, and we shared her agonized attempt to find him.   I remember Mr. Gifford said in a salute to our social caseworkers: "That is why we have you to help these lost ones in our big city."

The depression was deep, and our staff were overburdened with demands.   Appalled by the city turmoil and need, we helped create and staff the first Home Relief Department of the city to replace the outmoded out-door-relief program.   This work was a beginning part of the development of public welfare in our country.

Before the depression was over, much more needed doing through citizen action, and this is where our future bride, the Association for Improving the Condition of the Poor (AICP), played a leading part. Together our two then-separate agencies got the Gibson Emergency Relief Drive off to a spectacular start. Meantime AICP opened their Emergency Relief Bureau, where hundreds of unemployed received immediate financial help and jobs created through their public employment programs. Harry Hopkins, who was on their staff, felt the agony of the situation as he worked to help relieve it for many. Finally he was catapulted into the national effort, suggesting the Federal Emergency Relief Act (FERA) to President Franklin Roosevelt on the pattern of the New York effort.

Lucky for COS, too, that Mr. Gifford had the help of our new Executive Director, Stanley P. Davies, whose mental health and public welfare statewide experience made his appointment so pivotal to us. He and Bailey Burritt, the AICP executive, worked unsparingly in tandem during this dreadful period in our city's history.

My own part in this work was minor by comparison, Jeanie, but the suffering all around us and the exhaustion of our social work staff drove me to take some large-scale action on fund-raising and publicity. I decided not to stretch my efforts too thin but to concentrate on centers of power. I will give only two examples.

First, I decided to seek out as a representative of religion that great minister of

Riverside Church, Harry Emerson Fosdick. I did not know him but friends did. For our appointment I took along three real stories. I told him case by case what we were doing to help these and other people, especially the penniless heads of families whose jobs were first to go but who had not the health for WPA manual labor. I explained that we wanted to start a special employment center to find work for these blue-collar hard-to-place persons.

Dr. Fosdick, always a good listener and a man of deep feeling, took my *Bulletins* and offered to preach a sermon based on what I had told him. He would ask for a collection that Sunday to go entirely to starting such a special employment bureau. His wonderful presentation brought $5,000, to which his friend Dr. Russell Bowie, of Grace Christ Church, added $1,000. So our Kennedy Employment Service was born and operated for several years with their additional gifts and others until the State Employment Service could begin to handle the need.

Locating the next center of power was unplanned and exciting--*the theatre*. I went to see that wonderful actress Katharine Cornell, who was starring in *The Barretts of Wimpole Street*. And when the final curtain fell, I made a decision. I went backstage and asked to see her. There she was gracious and beautiful, welcoming me to her dressing room. I poured forth our story and the daily tales of suffering. Would she help us with a benefit even though we would have no time to sell tickets or help promote it?

She would, and what's more, as I rose to

go, she said: "Oh, how tired and wrung out
your social workers must be from the long hours
and inability to meet all the needs they see."

"Would it help," she added, "if I sent you
a block of free tickets to this play each week
so they and some of the persons they help could
have a bit of change and pleasure?" Typical it
was of this great lady, and there was great
staff pride that she cared so much and continued to send us tickets for such a long period.

I recalled all this to Miss Cornell in
1956, Jeanie, when I joined the staff of the
American Theatre Wing. Later on, through her
leadership and that of others, we formed Plays
for Living in 1959. I'll tell you more about
this, my last work venture, a little later.

Where was I? Oh, yes, telling you about
the big depression and my seeking out centers
of power in various fields to help us. It
occurred to me one day that it would hearten
and enliven our weary staff to hear about the
great woman, Josephine Shaw Lowell, who founded
COS in 1882, because the tragic depression of
those years gave her the inspiration to pioneer
in this way. So we invited our senior Board
member, a great civic leader, Charles C. Burlingham, who knew Mrs. Lowell personally, to
come and tell us about her.

One episode he gave was typical. He and
some ten other New York citizens who dominated
the news of that day were invited to her beautiful Staten Island home to dine. In the midst
of this dinner an idea came to her out of this
group's discussion. She later persuasively presented this idea to her friend Governor Roosevelt,

on whom she had called other times to press for what today we call "social action."

The COS staff members were electrified by Mr. Burlingham's memories of Mrs. Lowell and the great contributions she had made. He explained that the family had moved down from Boston so her mother could go to a famous eye specialist in New York. It was here that she and Robert W. de Forest became "allies." He admired her civic efforts, one of which resulted in the removal of children from almshouses where they were placed with adults, some insane. (Later COS founded the Children's Court.)

When you come to New York, Jeanie, I must take you to the foot of Bryant Park back of the 42nd Street Library, where you will see a bronze plaque dedicated to her. Honoring the founder of COS, it says: "She gave to it as long as her life lasted, her quickening spirit, her calm wisdom, and her all-embracing sympathy."

It was here as a Civil War widow that she tried to overcome her grief by seeking out others to help. She sat in this park and talked to ragged, unemployed veterans and others hit by the depression. As each told her his unique story, she became convinced that a voluntary movement to *help each individual according to his need*" was the only answer.

So it was out of her pioneering that COS was later born to give case-by-case attention to those in despair. A great New England abolitionist family, hers, and when you go to Boston, Jeanie, you will see on the Commons a monument to her brother, Robert Gould Shaw, on which there is the description of his death as the head of the first Negro regiment in the Civil War. It was of course in this same national conflict that Josephine Shaw Lowell's husband was killed not too long after their marriage. She had lost a distinguished man, kin of the poet James Russell Lowell, and a much beloved husband.

What a marvelous account of her Mr. Burlingham gave the staff that day. It lifted our sights and our hearts.

Mrs. Lowell's spirit seemed to go with me the next week when I visited Wellesley College to speak to the students about "Junior Month," which was soon to end as a project because the effect of the depression had become more widespread after the stock market crash of 1929. "Junior Month" could no longer claim the Society's funds when they were badly needed for depression use. So my enjoyable annual journeys to colleges ended with the Wellesley trip.

On the way home to New York I stopped off with a friend for the weekend at a nearby inn. It was the very next day, Saturday, March 4, 1933, that America took a new turn. All the inn's guests were invited to the dining room to hear Franklin Delano Roosevelt sworn into office as our next president. His ringing summons on the radio to have the courage for change was climaxed by his memorable challenge that we have nothing to fear but fear itself. The sound of his voice remains with me today when we face the need for such leadership to bring us together as a nation.

F.D.R.'s fearlessness two days later in closing all of the banks in the country to

prevent an oncoming panic brings me to remembering my return to New York after that weekend
when the banks were indeed closed and to the
realization that I had just ten dollars in cash.
But I had a brother--a dear lost-and-finally-
found brother--Captain Twining Tousley, whom
the doughboys affectionately called Pat as they
gathered around him in an Army hut near the
Marne in France. There he played to them as
they sang such World War I favorites as "Pack Up
Your Troubles in Your Old Kit Bag." This time
he helped me pack up *my* troubles, for he was
waiting in the apartment to give me $100 in
bills.

Next day I got myself to the office early
to see what was needed of me. It was plenty.
For the waiting room was filled with panicky
poor people. Our weary staff tried valiantly
during the days that followed to cope, as our
COS history records. Tragic depression years
those were that saw shabbily dressed business-
men selling apples on the street while head-
lines about bankruptcies that ended careers,
and even lives, were blazed across the press.

What a spell of sickness can do! For one thing, it can make history.

It was in the aftermath of the depression, in 1938, when illness struck down Walter Gifford, president of the Charity Organization Society, and Barklie Henry, president of the Association for Improving the Condition of the Poor. Meeting for the first time in the solarium of the New York Hospital during their convalescence, they became friends. Long talks about their social service responsibilities finally led to their conviction that a merger of these two old and distinguished family service agencies that they headed was desirable. Former studies had urged such a merger, but somehow it never materialized. So, with a postconvalescent bang, it did on April 12, 1939.

The search for a name for the new organization began. As fund-raiser for COS, I was somewhat chagrined but highly amused when one Trustee, Edward Streeter of *Father of the Bride* fame, suggested that the name be "the Association for Improving the Condition of the Poor Charity Organization Society." I bridled at that point and explained that COS had more individual donors than they did. But my AICP counterpart, Elsie Kearns, produced figures showing their preponderance of capital funds.

Finally, after the two Boards approved a merger, they agreed on the name, Community Service Society, and on the date, April 19, 1939, for a gala dinner at the Plaza Hotel for all the Trustees. The following morning the New York press would carry the whole newsworthy story about the merger of the two oldest and largest voluntary nonsectarian family agencies in the country, which had been going together-- and sometimes apart--since back in the nineteenth century.

On April 12 a small uprising took place. My staff counterpart and I advanced upon the executive directors of the two agencies, Stanley Davies and Bailey Burritt, both great men, and threw a monkey wrench into the plan for the Plaza dinner.

"You can't just spring the news of the merger on 750 staff members by letting them read about it in *The New York Times* the next morning or by leaving memos on their desks," we said. "Why can't the officers give them a big party too, perhaps the night before the Plaza affair, and have a whale of a welcome all around?"

The idea took root, and the following week at the old Murray Hill Hotel on 34th Street, a great old-time "sociable" took place, with the officers and staff executives taking turns at the mike after wet and dry punch bowls had been drained. I could hardly finish my own "broadcast" to the group, Jeanie, when I spied the New England-bred COS president sitting cozily on the floor with our department secretary, both quaffing away together in merry fashion.

So we were merged, and then began the exciting process of consolidation, not without pain at times. Especially do I remember that the temporary public relations man we had hired left all the announcement material he was to write up at a nudist camp, where he had spent the weekend. Somehow this crisis was surmounted.

Sometime before the Plaza announcement dinner I had been asked to meet with the two presidents about my part in the merged picture. Our conference at American Tel and Tel headquarters was formal and brief, during which I was offered the directorship of the Public Relations and Fund Raising Department for the merged agencies, with my counterpart, Miss Kearns, as assistant.

I remember asking the two officers, with some hesistancy, to whom I would report, realizing I would no longer be the Assistant General Director to Mr. Davies. Mr. Gifford's reply disturbed me greatly, for I was to be in the Comptroller's department. I argued that you couldn't interpret our professional programs to the public without participation in the policy-making and planning processes. "That's where ideas are born," I said.

Mr. Gifford, somewhat annoyed, suggested that I return to his inner office and think it over a few minutes while they settled other matters. I remember closing the door and standing by his wide window, through which I could see the Statue of Liberty shining in the bay in the sunset. I confess that I shed a tear over this difficult decision. I wiped it away and shortly returned to the outer office to tell them I was indeed honored but I could not accept. The two presidents were nonplussed, and indeed I was surprised at myself.

They asked, "Is it the money?" "No," I said, "your offer is generous; it's just that you can't function in a bookkeeping vacuum, far away from professional discussions and decision-making." I was excused from the conference and went home heartsick. I would be dropped from the staff, no doubt, and that night sleep refused to come. But, *mirabile dictu,* next day the matter was favorably settled. I would report to both parts of the agency. My suggestion of calling ours the Department of Public Interest, which I was to head, was approved, and a Public Interest Committee of the Board was appointed.

Jeanie, I should back up a bit from all this organizational story and tell you some things that happened to me on the personal side during this earlier period.

On August 18, 1926, a baby girl was born named Suzanne. She was immediately placed with a fine organization for adoption at the request of her very young teen-aged parents for reasons I do not know. In the end, when Suzanne was eighteen, she brought a richness to my life that nothing has surpassed.

It was July 4, 1945, when I first got acquainted with her. Very pretty, haughty, and disillusioned she was. By this time her elderly adoptive parents had died, leaving her with a trust fund but no trust, for she was homeless. Fortunately, family friends in this artists' town along the Delaware were temporarily boarding her until some plan could be made. I think destiny must have guided me to spend that holiday weekend with Margery Holmquist, a dear friend of mine who was close to Suzanne's situation.

I had no sooner put down my weekend bag when my hostess said, "You know, I hate to give you a busman's holiday from your job as a social worker, but nobody here knows what to do with Suzanne. She has been shuttled around so long from private schools to public ones while trust fund-appointed guardians tried unsuccessfully to handle the situation. "Understandably," Margery added, "she is now quite a young rebel.

"It is little wonder she has done poorly in schoolwork and even been expelled once. So I have asked my daughter, Christina, who is boarding her for the time being, to bring her over here tomorrow for you to talk to. Will you do it?"

So Suzy, as I call her, and I sat out on the grass under an apple tree. Immediately my heart went out to her. I never wanted to help anybody more, and yet every approach I made got nowhere. Feeling a complete failure, I abandoned anything a social worker would normally have said and blurted out, "You know, Suzy, I think you have had the goddamnedest childhood of anyone I ever knew."

"You do?" she asked with surprise. And then tears began to fall. "Well," she added, "there is nothing I or anybody can do about it." I can't remember if I hugged her to me at that point. I know I wanted to but feared she would pull away. But I did say, "Well, *I* know what to do about it," adding: "But it isn't true you can't do anything about it, for you have two great assets. I know about these from Aunt Margery, as you call her. She says you are wonderful with children and that you swim and dive like a little angel." Then I popped the question.

"When I go back to New York tomorrow, I think I can get you a job at a summer camp for poor children from broken homes who are even worse off than you are. Will you come," I asked, "if I can succeed?" She demurred, but finally said maybe she would.

The holiday train home was late, but when I got there I phoned my friend Margaret Barbee, the head of the New York Sheltering Arms, who lived in the same apartment house as I did. I asked her to come down to my apartment even though she had already gone to bed, adding, "This is a crisis." So we had a nightcap together and planned. She said their own summer camp might have a junior counselor vacancy. She would call the next morning, but it must be filled at once because camp had already opened.

By 10 a.m. I phoned Pennsylvania to tell Suzy the news. She said she wasn't sure she wanted to come because, "Oh, well . . ." "Come on, Suzy," I urged, "I will meet you at Penn Station. Yes, bring everything."

By noon there she was with a strange assortment of luggage and looking ever so young and vulnerable, but she knew I was deeply glad to see her. By afternoon she had deposited all her extras at my apartment and gone to the Sheltering Arms to pick up the two children she was to take up to their Connecticut camp on the late train.

"I hope I won't run away," she said to me as we got to Grand Central Station. She added, "I often do, but maybe I won't if you write me." So almost daily letters sped back and forth while a warm welcome from the older college counsellors buoyed her up and helped her to succeed.

Before the summer was over, I had made a plan she seemed to like--a plan that my friend Dr. Russell Bowie, a wonderful minister of Grace Church, had set in motion. Consequently, on Labor Day she moved into Grace Church House with other girls also arriving to study in New York. So what happened next?

You really think of amazing solutions, Jeanie, if you are a trained social worker. Our CSS had, I knew, recently opened a demonstration day nursery in Queens. So very shortly Suzy started a small paying job there helping with the children. She did so well that another, better paying one came along by the time she was nineteen.

Then came a bombshell! She told me she had decided she wanted a college education. "But, Suzy," I gasped, "of course you have your high school diploma. But, ye gods, you have a horrible academic record! Well," I added, "let's try it."

So once again I went back to my Sheltering Arms friend, who, I knew, was a Trustee of Stephens Junior College in Missouri. Luckily, President Wood was in town at the Biltmore, so we three were asked to breakfast with him. Before that I drew some money out of Suzy's trust fund, and up we went to De Pinna's, where chose an outfit that made her look irresistible, I thought.

Dr. Wood thought so too, for by the second cup of coffee, he told her the college would accept her on Miss Barbee's recommendation as a "special case" if she would make one promise. Suzy stiffened in readiness for a hard requirement, and he added, "You must not raid my icebox after midnight, for you and three other special students will be staying with me for the time being at the president's house."

At this point, Jeanie, perhaps I'd better make a long story short. Armed with a "B" average from Stephens, Suzy registered for her junior year at Whittier College in California, where they had a good course and field work in nursery school training.

It was June 1950 when I went out to her graduation. Upon her return to New York, she and three other girls and a cat took an apartment together. A new life and a new job began.

Did I forget to tell you that the night after her Whittier graduation, she sprung a whole new question on me of what to do about all these inner angers and problems that increasingly bedeviled her and made her lack a trust in people, particularly men?

After a long midnight talk, I finally said, "Suzy, you know there is a thing called psychoanalysis, which I think might be helpful. I could suggest one or two doctors if you ever wanted me to." I added my belief that her rocky road to life, along part of which we had stumbled together, would smooth out if she could come to terms with it--as I had been helped similarly by analysis.

Three months after that night she came to dinner at my New York apartment and almost imme-

diately said, "What's the name of that man?" I
knew whom she meant and gave her the phone number. Suzy made all her own arrangements, and
what a difference in her life came out of it all,
with real maturity and freedom from unbearable
inner doubts about herself and her background.

So in the end, Jeanie, she sailed off to
Germany to head a G.I. Service Men's Club near
Munich. There she met Fritz, a Plattling pho-
tographer, also on the Service Club staff. Yes,
you can guess what happened!

The first trans-Atlantic telephone call I
ever had was from Suzy, telling of her engage-
ment to Fritz--and asking if I would come over
to give her away. She insisted on paying my way
over out of her G.I. salary. Yes, I'd go, but
where on earth had I put my German textbook from
Oberlin College days? Ah, yes, I found it and
prepared a good speech to give Fritz's Bavarian
mother, whose hometown had been bombed by the
U.S., leaving her less than enthusiastic about
an American bride for her son. This feeling I
must dispel at all costs, so the moment I entered her door I delivered my greeting in poor
German, I am sure, but she hugged me and cried.
So did I. Then I gave her a Jensen pin I had
bought her as a token of our love for the family.

A lovely wedding followed on August 16,
1958, in the Niederalteich Cathedral. It was
unforgettable to Miss C.M.T., Suzy's godmother,
as I now called myself. I still remember her
wriggling her satin slippers as she knelt for
marriage. I remember me too, trying to wriggle
through a "bless you both" wedding speech at the
reception that followed.

After two champagnes and two dances with Fritz's brothers, my irregular verbs got horribly mixed up with German umlauts, but it didn't seem to matter. After their honeymoon we three met in Salzburg, to which lovely city I had returned from a ten-day sightseeing tour around Austria.

Why does it all mean so much? Well, I have two little "grandsons," Christopher and Peter, living not too far away, whose father chose America as his home in 1959, and Suzy, who seems like my own child. Lucky me! But, excuse me a minute, for I hear the phone ringing. A young voice from Colorado says, "Grandma, I'm in the sixth grade now, and we have a new dog, Rex."

At this point I must say *auf Wiedersehen* to them while I go back to where I left off telling you, Jeanie, about what happened next in my life.

Now to a noon session in 1947 of the Public Interest Committee and staff where we were reviewing the long-term results of the 1939 merger of AICP and COS before discussing proposed plans for the future.

It had been a civilized merger but painful. Some 80 Trustees and 700 professional and clerical staff were involved. These were two distinguished voluntary social agencies with roots deep in the last century, with different histories, different citizen and executive leadership, some leaders emphasizing the philanthropic and others the professional approach toward helping people out of trouble.

Both organizations sought very hard for a blend, and succeeded finally as an integrated force for the good of our city and for the spread of modern family social work throughout our country.

The adjustment years of the "marriage," however, were hard. They included the devastating World War II period ending in August 1945 (that saw also a few minor skirmishes within the agency). In a few years things were better all around.

Now the 1947 back-to-work noon session, I recall, discussed the public interest aspects of proposed plans for a 100th anniversary celebration. Exciting ideas had been submitted, which at this and many subsequent sessions were explored until solid plans were made.

The CSS Centennial took place at the Waldorf Astoria Hotel in the spring of 1948 and was a milestone in our history.

The Trustee Planning Committee, with our Public Interest help, had to keep two balls in the air in telling the story to the public. The first was, of course the CSS 100th, but the second, also important, was that the event included the 50th anniversary of the New York School of Social Work, the first of its kind in America. As one of the alumnae, I want to tell their part in the event first, and, anyway, shouldn't age bow to youth these days? Also, the school was still part of CSS until 1950, when its full affiliation with Columbia University was worked out.

I still like to review the history of the school's first session in the summer of 1898, for it illustrates dramatically the unique concept of the CSS movement from its beginning, namely, the essentiality of a partnership between citizen and professional leaders. It was the Friendly Visitors in New York and other cities who decided that their efforts as part-time volunteers were no longer sufficient to cope adequately with people's problems. These difficulties, they said, needed study as to causes so that better methods of helping could be created.

Then social workers could be trained to use these methods and improve on them as deeper insights resulted.

CSS President Robert W. de Forest, a great advocate of training, was the chief founder of the "Training Class in Philanthropy." Later, as president of the Russell Sage Foundation (which he got Mrs. Sage to set up), he was able to draw on its notable help in developing and housing the school through its early years.

In 1949 CSS had a wonderful invitation from the Carnegie Corporation. Would the school like to move to a landmark house--the former residence of Andrew Carnegie at 91st Street and Fifth Avenue (which offered a colorful garden for study and a pipe organ that wouldn't pipe)?

With my friend Margaret Leal, acting director of the school, I took the good old double-decker bus up Fifth Avenue to explore the possibilities. Could it be altered to accommodate classrooms and faculty offices?

We were met by the former Carnegie major domo, Manuel Perez, who showed us about while sandwiching in engaging interpolations. For instance, we asked, "Why the enormous bathtub alongside the smallish bedroom?" It would have held Prometheus I thought. "And why in Mr. Carnegie's study is there that outsize desk with a swivel chair behind it propped up on a platform?" The reply? "Well, you see, Mr. Carnegie was a little man sensitive about his size."

These comments were then quickly switched to Mrs. Carnegie, a "little lady who was adored --now this was the drawing room where she entertained so engagingly." The major domo next explained how he would stand beside her, announcing the names of the celebrities while Mrs. Carnegie greeted them with grace.

With a final look at the garden all in bloom, Margaret and I came back to mundane East 22nd Street saying, "Well, those were the nostalgic days of old New York, and surely the students will like studying among those memories even though the organ won't play again." Yes, they would--and did--from 1949 right up to the time of their final move to the Columbia University campus in 1971. Jeanie, the note the organ could strike if it would is that out of our small 1898 beginnings, 104 fellow schools across the country are, at this present date, graduating hundreds of much needed members for our profession.

Long ago someone described social workers as "shock absorbers of social change." That they are, in part at least, but more importantly they are social builders and preventers of needless family shock and disintegration. When will our nation resolve to produce more of these "builders?"

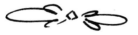

There were over 1,500 guests at the anniversary luncheon (I remember because I had to arrange the tricky protocol seating job). This event brought to a close the outstanding scientific and professional three-day symposium marking the 100th anniversary of the Community Service Society.

Speakers of national and international distinction included such men as Brock Chisholm speaking on "Human Relations on the World Scene," Harvard University's President James Conant on "Human Relations in Tomorrow's World," and Stuart Chase discussing "The Human Sciences and the Art of Practice."

All the leading papers were published in 1949 by the Columbia University Press. The one I remember best, perhaps because it applies so aptly to 1974 too, was that presented by the CSS General Director Stanley P. Davies, whose assistant I had been through the merger years and beyond. His final paragraph sums it up:

> Disdaining the paralysis of fear then, we need to be reinvigorated in our social efforts by the call from peoples everywhere to find the good life. . . . . Democracy has faith in people, in their ultimate wisdom and in their inherent desire and capacity to live and work together so as to achieve the fullest and richest life for all.

Great man that. A great year for me, Jeanie, of learning and helping right up to my 1955 retirement from CSS.

Somehow, as I contemplated my 1955 retirement, I could not see staying retired, so I went out the summer before to the University of California at Berkeley to teach a course in "Communications" at the School of Social Welfare.

It was hard, in a Berkeley garden where

morning finches sang to me and my view of the Golden Gate Bridge below and beautiful San Francisco kept enticing my eyes away from my notes, to program the course. But in the end this teacher was pleased to get an "A" from the administration in spite of weekends taken off to visit Lake Tahoe or explore Fisherman's Wharf in town.

Jeanie, you would have loved these jaunts that my faculty hostess, Gertrude Wilson, took me on, including a three-day sortie up the coast in her trailer. The whole summer experience strengthened me for the difficult 1955 CSS goodbyes at Christmas. And I was fortified, too, by knowing that I was leaving my post in the good hands of my chosen successor, Sallie Bright.

A great forty-three years it had been, during which both social work and I had a lot of growing up to do.

By 1955, Jeanie, some needed adrenalin was supplied to my energies by an invitation to join the staff of the prestigious, standard-setting Family Service Association of America (which CSS had "borned" in 1911 and which now boasted over 300 member agencies all over the U.S. and Canada).

It proved to be too brief a fund-raising gamble of a task because FSAA's fine leaders had mostly come out of local family service agencies, largely supported by fund-raising amalgams. Unlike CSS, these locals had not needed to learn the techniques of building a constituency of individual believers to support their agency's work and purposes.

CSS, to survive and grow, had to, and finally did, raise a family of some 15,000 contributors. They were thought of as partners in serving the community. In contrast, the national FSAA family was made up of dedicated member agencies. But I wanted these locals to have more citizen supporters of their own like CSS, and then to assist FSAA in organizing its own far-flung family of citizen givers.

Maybe an impossible dream, especially to accomplish in a hurry, and difficult in this day when bigness is king. Today, in looking back, the year with FSAA seems important to me, especially because I had the thrilling experience of learning much from the brilliant field staff that served every state in the Union with superb competence. Freda Burnside was one, and it was fun to raise all that money to start her off in Alaska. Allah be praised that Freda remained with FSAA and accomplished such fine things for the West Coast agencies and states, including Oregon. Jeanie, you will want to know more about her career. I sometimes see her as a modern-day Josephine Shaw Lowell in our national movement.

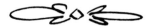

The curtain went up for me most thrillingly in 1957, Jeanie, when the American Theatre Wing invited me to become Public Interest Director of their Community Plays. The Plays grew out of the Wing's World War II Victory Plays, financed heavily by its Stage Door Canteen project. I was to help develop peacetime plays with a similar format and to contribute ideas on fund-raising.

I accepted with high enthusiasm because many of us at CSS had become firm believers that live theatre could bring the needs and purposes of the Society, as well as other helping agencies, home to the people better than the best of speeches or written reports.

We especially found the audience discussion period that followed each half-hour performance to be a dynamic source of group learning, whether the audience was made up of contributors at a Waldorf Astoria luncheon or PTA members at a public school or people at some church gathering. (We played the night of the Big Blackout before candles on the altar of the Park Avenue Methodist Church, thinking it was a blown fuse causing the sudden darkness. We learned later that this was the only theatre to perform in New York that night.)

There were myriad problems besetting New York after the war was over which needed community understanding. That was why the Wing's Community Plays Committee, under Vera Allen, went into high gear. For one thing, they induced the Grant Foundation, through Adele Morrison, to underwrite a promotion post at the Wing for me.

The new job began July 1, 1957. With the aid from the start of a strong Advisory Committee that included Vera Allen, Margaret Mead, Nina Ridenour, and actress Jeanie Chapel, it was a heady time for me. As a bona fide staff member of the prestigious Wing, I could with confidence use all the local and national contacts I had ever made during my professional years at CSS.

It emboldened me right off to wangle a date in Washington with Mary Switzer, Director of Vocational Rehabilitation with the Department of Health, Education, and Welfare. A theatre buff herself, she was immediately full of ideas about the problems they faced that could be dramatized to gain public understanding. Before we were through with the session, she had commissioned

The Picnic Basket and promised others if the
first one succeeded.   This one, written by our
well-known author Nora Stirling, concerned the
rough road that a former mental patient must
travel when he leaves the hospital and returns
to the normal work-a-day world--an impossible
journey without the understanding and help of
his fellow men.

We had a tryout of it before some fifty patients who were going home the next day.   Their
relatives also were invited to see the play by
Dr. Diamond, the psychiatrist in charge.   Our
actors were tense, as were the patients, so Dr.
Diamond asked the audience for only a few comments after the curtain went down.

I couldn't hold back the tears, Jeanie,
when the first patient arose to say: "This
play teaches me that if you go home with your
head high and your self-respect intact you will
have won the most important first step, after
which the rest will be easier."   She was loudly
applauded by the audience.   So I cried, for it
was a moving experience for anybody "on the
outside."

The four other plays Miss Switzer commissioned for nationwide performances were equally
successful and are still in our repertory.

Encouraged by my Washington success with
H.E.W., I had growing confidence in our future
but realized, as did the Wing's president, that
we needed a strong Public Interest Committee of
lay and theatre members if we were to meet the
changed situation now that war funds were no
longer available and peacetime financing as well
as peacetime plays were needed.

Convinced that our CSS Board member Mrs. C. Reynolds Pratt would ideally fill the bill as chairman, Vera Allen and I called on her to extend the Wing's invitation. Fortunately, she accepted the appointment to set up a Public Interest Committee of broad influence. With her infectious enthusiasm she soon enlisted a wonderful group.

Katharine Cornell became cochairman, and such theatre and lay leading figures as Cornelia Otis Skinner, Mrs. J. Campbell Burton, Gertrude Macy, Mrs. Richard Bernhard, and Mrs. David Levy were added. It was easy to help them use their prestige with their various contacts to raise foundation money and sizable contributor gifts while obtaining commissions for new plays and initiating performances before their church groups, college alumnae audiences, and social agency annual meetings.

Meantime there was the fun of being in on the building of each new play. The "builders" included the special writer we had chosen, the professionals of the agency commissioning the play, and, sometimes, their clients. This panel, with various representatives of our Public Interest Committee, often had knowledgeable outsiders added to it. The creative process of building a play was as fascinating an experience as one can have. The commissioning agency would first be asked, "What is it you mostly wish to get across to the public in this half-hour play?" Out of the group discussion that followed came a rich cross-fertilization of ideas.

There were many uproariously funny times too. Often our theatre members would say, "You are outlining material for a three-hour play, not thirty minutes"; or another would chip in with, "Your central idea is not drama, but that other one you described a while back--that is high theatre."

Once in the garden at Judge Justine Wise Polier's home, when we were discussing a delinquency play for the National Association on Crime and Delinquency, I remember our executive producer, Ethel Barrymore Colt, exploding with: "Everybody's too nice in your proposed play--the mother, the probation officer, and the judge; we need a villain or an obnoxious character of some sort."

To this Judge Polier replied: "Okay. Let's have the judge be the stupid one--at least until the light dawns on him." The resulting play, *A Shirt a Size Too Small,* is still being performed before responsive audiences to whom the boy who stole the red shirt has great appeal.

Community Plays grew like Topsy on the mid-eastern seaboard, where resources for acting groups and audiences were within reach. (Within the fifty-mile area of New York we used our own Equity players.)

What we now needed most was some tie-up that would give us access to groups across the nation. We thought about organizing chapters of Community Plays, but this was too ambitious an idea for our limited staff and funds. This growing problem and changes at the American

Theatre Wing by the spring of 1958 made us receptive to an invitation from the Family Service Association of America to join them, using their 350 local family agencies throughout the country as outlets for our plays.

This shift of auspices, meeting with the approval of the Wing's president, was accomplished in the fall of 1958.

On January 1, 1959, we became an official division of FSAA operating from their national headquarters in New York. Months of planning were involved, but first we had to create a new name for our project, and finally Plays for Living was chosen. As its executive director I was able, having worked with many FSAA local agencies, rather quickly to stir up national interest in the use of our plays. Many of the agencies had their own local players or college drama groups to rely on. Some organized Plays for Living committees to promote local and state performances.

One important piece of advice we gave them: "Be sure you choose a discussion leader who knows the field portrayed by the play, but equally important be sure the moderator can bring out a free-wheeling discussion and not dominate it with his or her own conclusions, thus freezing participation."

Social workers were sometimes the worst

sinners. That dedicated Jane Hoey, from the
Federal Social Security Agency of long ago, had
such concern for people on welfare that after
our play on the subject she said hotly while
leading the discussion, "That just isn't so!"--
instead of using our suggested handling of carp-
ing critics by saying, "Okay, now what do some
of the rest of you think; do you all agree with
this lady?"

Plays for Living in the next decade expand-
ed rapidly under the growing leadership of our
prestigious Board, headed by Mrs. Pratt and
Katharine Cornell. By the early 1970s we had
an exciting repertory of some fifty plays and an
imposing group of commissioning agencies. On
the national level these included:

American Association of Retired Persons
Department of Health, Education, and Welfare
National Council of Christians and Jews
National Travelers Aid Association
National Council on Crime and Delinquency
Child Study Association of America
American Red Cross
American Cancer Society
National Council on Alcoholism

We also had attracted some seventy-five patrons paying $100 yearly--a real constituency to
undergird Plays for Living.

It was hard for me, I must confess, to
"hang loose" when it came time to step down to
the post of half-time consultant. Finally, on
June 1, 1970, I retired entirely to become executive director emeritus of the Plays, leaving
the project in the competent hands of our new
executive director, Mrs. Ann Booth.

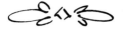

A creative venture it was, Jeanie, using the theatre to get across to the public the tested findings of many grass-roots professionals. Personally too, it gave me the golden opportunity to carry out my earlier conviction that "pros," working in tandem with Board and other citizen leaders, can do wonders. They can not only provide a most effective way to attract knowledgeable support, but also can get the public thinking more deeply about people with problems, even going to bat for them one way or another. Such recognized spokesmen can open new doors that staff cannot.

For instance, the time our Plays for Living chairman enticed her friends Fredric March and Florence Eldridge, famous husband-and-wife acting team, to invite friends to their home to see a play of ours. Some of the guests later became patrons, and all of them that night participated in the thought-provoking discussion that followed the performance. New doors, new understanding.

The pattern worked over and over through the years. For instance, it worked later on at an unforgettable gathering of guests at the home of Mrs. Bernard F. Gimbel, when a distinguished integrated cast performed *The Man Nobody Saw*, after which the late Whitney Young, Jr., executive director of the National Urban League, led the audience discussion.

Lively and frank it was, for this distinguished man provided an atmosphere that fostered thinking aloud together. What an experience! I wish you could have been there, Jeanie. People pondered and listened and learned.

Not only Plays for Living, but also at an earlier time at CSS, Board members similarly enjoyed the tandem approach where they, on occasion, could pick up a staff idea about some top contact of theirs and, provided with the material to use, could go to town on it to the delight of staff. So it was with our half-hour dramas that we played to prominent citizens as well as to the equally important but less favored of our city.

Real communication resulted wherever we went. John Steinbeck described this result in *Travels with Charley,* when he wrote about a man he and his dog Charley met at a North Dakota camping spot--an actor who was doing one-night stands. Steinbeck called the actor's profession "one older than writing and one that will survive when the written word has disappeared." He added: "All the sterile wonders of movies, television and radio will fail to wipe it out-- a living man in communication with a living audience."

Plays for Living and other visual arts besides theatre have a spiraling contribution to make today when communication gets too "instant." On the one hand the public has the valuable but capsulized media to inform them about people and problems and, on the other, a surfeit of lengthy professional or intellectualized reading material--so they go off to play bridge when it gets too much.

Not so with a play like *The Man Nobody Saw*

and others in our repertory. They grab your heart and mind and then allow you to speak up. New ideas about old dilemmas emerge later to be taken advantage of in one's family life or community. Ours are plays for living in every sense, and that is why I was delighted when the name occurred to me.

To keep democracy functioning in our wonderful, diverse nation, we need to listen to each other more and try to understand and utilize differences. The *Literary Digest* of October 18, 1930, put it best: "Mutual appreciation is the culminating virtue of a civilized society--not a melting pot, but an orchestration."

To you, Jeanie, I'd say that the sixty years in social work gave me a privileged education in living. You learn that people are just people and that artificial pedestals don't really count much. As a caseworker I found often that the members of the simplest homes were the most gifted in the art of parenthood and family life. We learned from them.

We found, too, many notable people of high business status that showed America at its democratic best. They gave an open kind of leadership that filtered right down to their littlest employees, and they liked the tandem ways of the helping professions.

Long ago, when I was rushing to Madison Square Garden to hear Adlai Stevenson speak, my taxi driver said approvingly, "I hear him on the air and I like him." When I asked why, he hesitatingly said, "I guess it is because he has 'intrigity'"--and then he added, "I didn't say that right, did I, but you know what I mean." Indeed I did, and I said so.

Whether you go into medicine or social work,

Jeanie, remember psychiatrist Kubie's advice to his coprofessionals: "Don't retreat from people." Mass action is the thing of the day right now, and some of it is needed to be sure. But a heightened concern for the individual, with his different needs and strengths, must remain strong if "intrigity" in our national life is to prevail.

Good family life is where it all begins. It is central to the well-being of every growing person. One's hunger for it is basic and is most apparent in the disappointed young people who then try to make "a family" out of their peers or others. They want to belong; so, Jeanie, help them.

NOTES ABOUT THE LETTER-WRITER

Clare M. Tousley
235 East 22nd Street
New York, New York 10010

1889:   Born December 25 in Warren, Illinois.

1911:   B.A. degree, Oberlin College; LL.D.
         degree, 1937.

1911-12: Taught first grade at Minnesota State
         School for Dependent Children.

1912:   On December 20 joined the staff of the
         Charity Organization Society.

1917:   M.A. degree, New York School of Phi-
         lanthropy.

1919:   On September 22 was appointed to COS
         headquarters; published early *Bul-
         letin* as C.M.T., Editor; developed
         and directed "Junior Month" (1920-
         33), attended by a representative
         from each of twelve women's col-
         leges; taught social work to Bar-
         nard College seniors; became COS
         Director of Volunteers; appointed
         Assistant Director of COS for pub-
         lic relations, fund-raising, and
         Board development; became Director
         of the Department of Public Inter-
         est, CSS, after COS-AICP merger in
         April 1939.

1926-46: Taught Junior League provisional
         course; chaired Advisory Committee.

1955:   Retired from CSS on December 31.
         Taught "Communications" course at
         School of Social Welfare, Univer-
         sity of California at Berkeley.

1956:   Joined Family Service Association of
           America staff to help in develop-
           ment and fund-raising.
1957:   Became Public Interest Director, Com-
           munity Plays, American Theatre
           Wing.
1958:   With Charlotte Pratt and Vera Allen
           formed Plays for Living, which be-
           came a division of FSAA.
1958-67:   Executive Director, Plays for Living;
           helped obtain commissions, nation-
           wide performances with the backing
           of such stars on the PFL Committee
           as Katharine Cornell, Peggy Wood,
           Cornelia Otis Skinner, and Ethel
           Barrymore Colt.
1967:   Became Special Consultant to Plays for
           Living, retiring in 1970 to become
           Executive Director Emeritus.

Memberships: Honorary life member, New York Ju-
              nior League; life member, National
              Conference on Social Welfare, New
              York State Welfare Conference;
              honorary member and a founder
              (1922), National Association of
              Social Workers; member, Women's
              City Club, League of Women Voters,
              National Urban League, National
              Association for the Advancement of
              Colored People, American Civil
              Liberties Union, Common Cause.